W9-BLZ-254

THE
JOURNAL
OF
MADAM KNIGHT

SARAH KEMBLE KNIGHT

APPLEWOOD BOOKS

BEDFORD, MASSACHUSETTS

The Journal of Madam Knight was originally published in 1825.

ISBN: 1-55709-115-3

Thank you for purchasing an Applewood book. Applewood reprints America's lively classics— books from the past that are still of interest to modern readers. For a free copy of our current catalog, please write to Applewood Books, 18 North Road, Bedford, MA 01730.

10 9 8 7 6 5 4 3 2

Library of Congress Cataloging-in-Publication Data
Knight, Sarah Kemble, 1666-1727.
    The journal of Madam Knight / Sarah Kemble Knight.
            p.   cm.
    Originally published by Theodore Dwight of New York in 1825.
    ISBN 1-55709-115-3
    1. New England—Description and travel—To 1775.   I. Title.
F7.K724   1992
917.404'202—dc20   91-46984
    [B]   CIP

THE

JOURNAL

OF

Madam KNIGHT

With an INTRODUCTORY NOTE by
GEORGE PARKER WINSHIP

BOSTON:

Printed by BRUCE ROGERS for the Publishers

SMALL, MAYNARD & COMPANY

1920

Introductory Note.

MADAM KNIGHT'S Journal is the truest picture left to us of provincial New England. Ever since it was first printed in 1825 it has been the delight of those whose reading takes them below the surface of current writings about colonial times, but it has nevertheless remained one of the least familiar of contemporary sources. The reason for this may have something to do with the fact that the people described by her are not like those portrayed in most of the books about ancestral New Englanders.

The Journal was written midway of the hundred years during which the primitive settlements developed into readiness for independence. The writer was a lady of good family in respectable social and church standing, who was much too busy with the affairs of daily life to concern herself unduly with matters of state or of religion. It is this absorption in her immediate surroundings which gives perennial fascination to her account of a trip on horseback from Boston to New York. The people with whom she had to do on the way and the things they talked about were neither deacons nor Heaven, but both were typical of the period during which were established the New England characteristics which have had an influence upon the United States.

Sarah Kemble Knight was thirty-eight years old when she made the fearsome journey along the route now followed by the "Shore Line" trains. She was the daughter of a Charlestown shop-keeper who appears not to have bettered himself by moving across the river to Boston. There she married the American agent for a merchant in London, where her husband died after a prolonged absence from home. While he was overseas, she occupied herself in various remunerative ways. She taught the youngsters of the neighborhood, among whom tradition named the Mathers and Ben Franklin, to write, and her skill with the pen was utilized by those having letters to compose, court records to copy, or legal documents to draft.

Her house near the North Square, the center
of the residential section of the town, had
been purchased by her father, but it reverted
later to the estate of the family from which
he bought it. There she kept a shop, and the
records state that it was also the residence
of a relative by marriage and of two or three
others who it is fair to conjecture were paying guests.

One member of this household was a
young widow, the daughter of a politician
who held office under the General Court.
She found a second husband in July, 1704,
in Madam Knight's well-to-do cousin, Caleb
Trowbridge of New Haven. Presumably he
had come to Boston to visit his relatives, or
maybe seeking medical advice. The scanty
recorded facts are quite enough to set the
imagination guessing at the many things
that must have happened in that North End
boarding-house presided over by the plump
mistress whose independent mind and ener-
getic, withal somewhat feminist, character
compensated for whatever she may have
lacked of fortune. Early in September the
bride was again a widow, and three weeks

later Madam Knight started for New Haven. Her business there had to do with the settlement of the estate, and when Caleb's father, her kinsman Thomas Trowbridge, decided to keep her waiting until he had been to New York, she likewise decided to go there with him. The inevitable inference gives rise to another surmise, that her familiarity with legal documents, of which the court files contain many in what is thought to be her handwriting, enabled her to undertake the work of a lawyer in looking after the interests of the recently widowed Mrs. Trowbridge.

During her journey the traveller was accustomed to set down her daily observations the last thing before retiring. There is nothing improbable in the statement that she did this in shorthand, and that her diary contained much more than appears in the printed copy. This was first published by Theodore Dwight of New York from a manuscript "neatly copied into a small book," but whether it was in Madam Knight's hand is not clear. Mr. Dwight secured it from a descendant of Sarah Christophers, the relative who administered the estate of the diarist's only daughter. All but a single leaf had disappeared before 1858, when William R. Deane saw it while preparing to write an introduction to a reprint of the Journal, in *Littell's Living Age* for that year. It had previously been printed in the Boston weekly *Protestant Telegraph* for 1847. Two other separate editions have appeared, at Albany, N.Y., in 1865, and at Norwich, Connecticut, in 1901. The anonymous notes in the Albany reprint were supplied by Judge William L. Learned. The Norwich edition, for which Henry W. Kent was largely responsible, was the handiwork of two local institutions, the manual training department of the Free Academy and the Norwich Art School. It contains Mr. Deane's introduction of 1858 with an explanatory note by Robert P. Keep and a commendatory page contributed by Donald G. Mitchell. A paper by Rev. Anson Titus, printed in volume ix, 1912, of the *Bostonian Society Publications*, brings together the little additional information that has been published about Madam Sarah Knight and her connections.

As the introductions to the preceding

editions comment on the progressive short-
ening of the time taken to make the journey from Boston to New York at the dates
of their respective issues, it may be well to
quote Mr. Deane's statement, in 1858, that
"we are usually whirled over the ground in
about eight hours, and it has been accomplished in five." The wise editor of 1865,
noting that the "time is now reduced to
eight hours," ventured to "think that the
speed of travel will never be carried to a
much higher degree."

G. P. W.

1920

THE PRIVATE JOURNAL

KEPT BY

Madam *KNIGHT*,

On a Journey

From BOSTON *to* NEW-YORK,

In the Year 1704.

From the Original Manuscript.

INTRODUCTION

To the Edition of 1825.

By Theodore Dwight.

THIS *is not a work of fiction, as the scarcity of old American manuscripts may induce some to imagine; but it is a faithful copy from a diary in the author's own hand-writing, compiled soon after her return home, as it appears, from notes recorded daily, while on the road. She was a resident of Boston, and a lady of uncommon literary attainments, as well as of great taste and strength of mind. She was called Madam Knight, out of respect to her character, according to a custom once common in New England; but what was her family name the publishers have not been able to discover.*

The object proposed in printing this little work is not only to please those who have particularly studied the progressive history of our country, but to direct the attention of others to subjects of that description, unfashionable as they still are; and also to remind the public that documents, even as unpretending as the following, may possess a real value, if they contain facts which will be hereafter sought for to illustrate interesting periods in our history.

It is to be regretted that the brevity of the work should have allowed the author so little room for the display of the cultivated mind and the brilliant fancy which frequently betray themselves in the course of the narrative; and no one can rise from the perusal without wishing some happy chance might yet discover more full delineations of life and character from the same practised hand.

Subjects so closely connected with ourselves ought to excite a degree of curiosity and interest, while we are generally so ready to open our minds and our libraries to the most minute details of foreign governments, and the modes and men of distant countries, with which we can have only a collateral connection.

In copying the following work for the press, the original orthography has been carefully preserved, in some cases, it may be, so far as to retain the errors of the pen, for fear of introducing any unwarrantable modernism. The punctuation was very hasty, and therefore has not been regarded.

Two interruptions occur in the original near the commencement, which could not be supplied; and in a few instances it has been thought proper to make short omissions, but none of them materially affect the narrative.

The reader will find frequent occasion to compare the state of things in the time of our author with that of the present period, par-

ticularly with regard to the number of the inhabitants, and the facilities and accommodations prepared for travellers. Over that tract of country where she travelled about a fortnight, on horseback, under the direction of a hired guide, with frequent risks of life and limb, and sometimes without food or shelter for many miles, we proceed at our ease, without exposure and almost without fatigue, in a day and a half, through a well peopled land, supplied with good stage-coaches and public houses, or the still greater luxuries of the elegant steam boats which daily traverse our waters.

THE
J O U R N A L
OF
Madam *KNIGHT*.

❖❖❖❖❖❖❖❖❖❖❖❖❖❖❖❖❖❖❖❖

Monday, Octb'r. yᵉ second,
1704.

ABOUT three o'clock afternoon, I
begun my Journey from Boſton
to New-Haven; being about two Hundred Mile. My Kinsman, Capt. Robert
Luiſt, waited on me as farr as Dedham,
where I was to meet yᵉ Weſtern poſt.

I

I vissitted the Reverd. Mr. Belcher, yᵉ Miniſter of yᵉ town, and tarried there till evening, in hopes yᵉ poſt would come along. But he not coming, I resolved to go to Billingses where he used to lodg, being 12 miles further. But being ignorant of the way, Madᵐ Billings,* seing no persuasions of her good spouses or hers could prevail with me to Lodg there that night, Very kindly went wyth me to yᵉ Tavern, where I hoped to get my guide, And desired the Hoſtess to inquire of her gueſts whether any of them would go with mee. But they, being tyed by the Lipps to a pewter engine, scarcely allowed themselves time to say what clownish . . . .

Evidently this should be "Madᵐ Belcher"

❀❀❀❀❀❀❀❀❀❀❀❀❀❀❀❀❀

Here half a page of the MS. is gone.

❀❀❀❀❀❀❀❀❀❀❀❀❀❀❀❀❀

. . . . Peices

. . . . Peices of eight, I told her no, I would not be accessary to such extortion.

Then John shan't go, sais shee. No, indeed, shan't hee; And held forth at that rate a long time, that I began to fear I was got among the Quaking tribe, beleeving not a Limbertong'd siſter among them could out do Madm. Hoſtes.

Upon this, to my no small surprise, son John arrose, and gravely demanded what I would give him to go with me? Give you, sais I, are you John? Yes, says he, for want of a Better; And behold! this John look't as old as my Hoſt, and perhaps had bin a man in the laſt Century. Well, Mr. John, sais I, make your demands. Why, half a pss. of eight and a dram, sais John. I agreed, and gave him a Dram (now) in hand to bind the bargain.

My hoſtess catechis'd John for going

so

so cheap, saying his poor wife would break her heart . . .

❀❀❀❀❀❀❀❀❀❀❀❀❀❀❀❀❀❀❀❀❀❀

Here another half page of the MS. is gone.

❀❀❀❀❀❀❀❀❀❀❀❀❀❀❀❀❀❀❀❀❀❀

. . . His shade on his Hors resembled a Globe on a Gate poſt. His habitt, Hors and furniture, its looks and goings Incomparably answered the reſt.

Thus Jogging on with an easy pace, my Guide telling mee it was dangero's to Ride hard in the Night, (wh^ch his hors had the sence to avoid,) Hee entertained me with the Adventurs he had passed by late Rideing, and eminent Dangers he had escaped, so that, Remembring the Hero's in Parismus and the Knight of the Oracle, I didn't know but I had mett wth a Prince disguis'd.

When we had Ridd about an how'r, wee

wee come into a thick swamp, wch. by Reason of a great fogg, very much startled mee, it being now very Dark. But nothing dismay'd John: Hee had encountered a thousand and a thousand such Swamps, having a Universall Knowledge in the woods; and readily Answered all my inquiries wch. were not a few.

In about an how'r, or something more, after we left the Swamp, we come to Billinges, where I was to Lodg. My Guide dismounted and very Complasantly help't me down and shewd the door, signing to me wth his hand to Go in; wch I Gladly did——But had not gone many steps into the Room, ere I was Interogated by a young Lady I understood afterwards was the Eldest daughter of the family, with these, or words to this purpose, (*viz.*) Law for mee——what in the world brings You here at this time a night?——I never see a woman on the Rode so Dreadfull late, in all the days of my versall life. Who are You? Where are You going? I'me scar'd out of my witts—with much now of the same Kind. I stood aghast, Prepareing to reply, when in comes my Guide—to him Madam turn'd, Roreing out: Lawfull heart, John, is it You?—how de do! Where in the world are you going with this woman? Who is she? John made no Ansr. but sat down in the corner, fumbled out his black Junk, and saluted that instead of Debb; she then turned agen to mee and fell anew into her silly questions, without asking mee to sitt down.

I told her shee treated me very Rudely, and I did not think it my duty to answer her unmannerly Questions. But to get ridd of them, I told her I come there to have the post's company with me to-morrow on my Journey, &c. Miss
Star'd

Star'd awhile, drew a chair, bid me sitt,
And then run upStairs and putts on two
or three Rings, (or else I had not seen
them before,) and returning, sett herself juSt before me, showing the way to
Reding, that I might see her Ornaments,
perhaps to gain the more respeСt. But
her Granam's new Rung sow, had it appeared, would affeСted me as much. I
paid honeSt John wth money and dram
according to contraСt, and DismiSt him,
and pray'd Miss to shew me where I
muSt Lodg. Shee conduСted me to a
parlour in a little back Lento, wch was
almoSt fill'd wth the bedSted, wch was so
high that I was forced to climb on a chair
to giu up to ye wretched bed that lay
on it; on wch having Stretcht my tired
Limbs, and lay'd my head on a Sad-col-
ourd pillow, I began to think on the
transaСtions of ye paSt day.

Tuesday,

※※※※※※※※※※※※※※※※※※※

Tuesday, October ye third,

about 8 in the morning, I with the Post proceeded forward without observing any thing remarkable; And about two, afternoon, Arrived at the Post's second Stage, where the western Post mett him and exchanged Letters. Here, having called for something to eat, ye woman bro't in a Twisted thing like a cable, but something whiter; and laying it on the bord, tugg'd for life to bring it into a capacity to spread; wch having wth great pains accomplished, she serv'd in a dish of Pork and Cabage, I suppose the remains of Dinner. The sause was of a deep Purple, wch I tho't was boil'd in her dye Kettle; the bread was Indian, and every thing on the Table service Agreeable to these. I, being hungry,

hungry, gott a little down; but my Stomach was soon cloy'd, and what cabbage I swallowed serv'd me for a Cudd the whole day after.

Having here discharged the Ordnary for self and Guide, (as I underStood was the cuStom,) About Three, afternoon, went on with my Third Guide, who Rode very hard; and having crossed Providence Ferry, we come to a River wch they Generally Ride thro'. But I dare not venture; so the PoSt got a Ladd and Cannoo to carry me to tother side, and hee rid thro' and Led my hors. The Cannoo was very small and shallow, so that when we were in she seem'd redy to take in water, which greatly terrified mee, and caused me to be very circumspect, sitting with my hands faSt on each side, my eyes Stedy, not daring so much as to lodg my tongue a hair's breadth more on one side of my mouth than tother,

tother, nor so much as think on Lott's wife, for a wry thought would have oversett our wherey: But was soon put out of this pain, by feeling the Cannoo on shore, wch I as soon almost saluted with my feet; and Rewarding my sculler, again mounted and made the best of our way forwards. The Rode here was very even and ye day pleasant, it being now near Sunsett. But the Post told mee we had neer 14 miles to Ride to the next Stage, (where we were to Lodg.) I askt him of the rest of the Rode, foreseeing wee must travail in the night. Hee told mee there was a bad River we were to Ride thro', wch was so very firce a hors could sometimes hardly stem it: But it was but narrow, and wee should soon be over. I cannot express the concern of mind this relation sett me in: no thoughts but those of the dang'ros River could entertain my Imagination, and

and they were as formidable as varios, still Tormenting me with blackest Ideas of my Approching fate——Sometimes seing my self drowning, otherwhiles drowned, and at the best like a holy Sister Just come out of a Spiritual Bath in dripping Garments.

Now was the Glorious Luminary, wth his swift Coursers arrived at his Stage, leaving poor me wth the rest of this part of the lower world in darkness, with which wee were soon Surrounded. The only Glimering we now had was from the spangled Skies, Whose Imperfect Reflections rendered every Object formidable. Each lifeless Trunk, with its shatter'd Limbs, appear'd an Armed Enymie; and every little stump like a Ravenous devourer. Nor could I so much as discern my Guide, when at any distance, which added to the terror.

Thus, absolutely lost in Thought, and dying

dying with the very thoughts of drowning, I come up with the Post, who I did
not see till even with his Hors: he told
mee he stopt for mee; and wee Rode on
Very deliberatly a few paces, when we
entred a Thickett of Trees and Shrubbs,
and I perceived by the Hors's going, we
were on the descent of a Hill, w^{ch}, as wee
come neerer the bottom, 'twas totaly dark
wth the Trees that surrounded it. But I
knew by the Going of the Hors wee had
entred the water, wch my Guide told mee
was the hazzardos River he had told me
off; and hee, Riding up close to my Side,
Bid me not fear—we should be over Im-
ediatly. I now ralyed all the Courage I
was mistriss of, Knowing that I must
either Venture my fate of drowning,
or be left like ye Children in the wood.
So, as the Post bid me, I gave Reins to my
Nagg; and sitting as Stedy as Just before
in the Cannoo, in a few minutes got safe

to

to the other side, which hee told mee was the Narragansett country.

Here We found great difficulty in Travailing, the way being very narrow, and on each side the Trees and bushes gave us very unpleasent welcomes wth their Branches and bow's, wch wee could not avoid, it being so exceeding dark. My Guide, as before so now, putt on harder than I, wth my weary bones, could follow; so left mee and the way beehind him. Now Returned my distressed aprehensions of the place where I was: the dolesome woods, my Company next to none, Going I knew not whither, and encompased wth Terrifying darkness; The least of which was enough to startle a more Masculine courage. Added to which the Reflections, as in the afternoon of ye day that my Call was very Questionable, wch till then I had not so Prudently as I ought considered. Now, coming

coming to ye foot of a hill, I found great difficulty in ascending; But being got to the Top, was there amply recompenced with the friendly Appearance of the Kind Conductress of the night, Just then Advancing above the Horisontall Line. The Raptures wch the Sight of that fair Planett produced in mee, caus'd mee, for the Moment, to forgett my present wearyness and past toils; and Inspir'd me for most of the remaining way with very divirting tho'ts, some of which, with the other Occurances of the day, I reserved to note down when I should come to my Stage. My tho'ts on the sight of the moon were to this purpose:

Fair Cynthia, all the Homage that I may
Unto a Creature, unto thee I pay;
In Lonesome woods to meet so kind a guide,
To Mee's more worth than all the world beside.
Some Joy I felt just now, when safe got or'e
Yon Surly River to this Rugged shore, [Trees
Deeming Rough welcomes from these clownish
Better than Lodgings wth Nereidees.

                                  Yet

Yet swelling fears surprise; all dark appears—
Nothing but Light can disipate those fears.
My fainting vitals can't lend strength to say,
But softly whisper, O I wish 'twere day.
The murmer hardly warm'd the Ambient air,
E're thy Bright Aspect rescues from dispair:
Makes the old Hagg her sable mantle loose,
And a Bright Joy do's through my Soul diffuse.
The Boistero's Trees now Lend a Passage Free,
And pleasent prospects thou giv'st light to see.

From hence wee kept on, with more ease yⁿ before: the way being smooth and even, the night warm and serene, and the Tall and thick Trees at a distance, especially wⁿ the moon glar'd light through the branches, fill'd my Imagination wᵗʰ the pleasent delusion of a Sumpteous citty, fill'd wᵗʰ famous Buildings and churches, wᵗʰ their spiring steeples, Balconies, Galleries and I know not what: Granduers wᶜʰ I had heard of, and wᶜʰ the ſtories of foreign countries had given me the Idea of.

Here

Here stood a Lofty church—there is a steeple,
And there the Grand Parade—O see the people!
That Famouse Castle there, were I but nigh,
To see the mote and Bridg and walls so high—
They'r very fine! sais my deluded eye.

Being thus agreably entertain'd without a thou't of any thing but thoughts themselves, I on a suden was Rous'd from these pleasing Imaginations, by the Post's sounding his horn, which assured mee hee was arrived at the Stage, where we were to Lodg: and that musick was then most musickall and agreeable to mee.

Being come to mr. Havens', I was very civilly Received, and courteously entertained, in a clean comfortable House; and the Good woman was very active in helping off my Riding clothes, and then ask't what I would eat. I told her I had some Chocolett, if shee would prepare it; which with the help of some Milk, and a little clean brass Kettle, she soon

soon effected to my satisfaction. I then
betook me to my Apartment, wch was
a little Room parted from the Kitchen
by a single bord partition; where, after
I had noted the Occurrances of the past
day, I went to bed, which, tho' pretty
hard, Yet neet and handsome. But I
could get no sleep, because of the Clam-
or of some of the Town tope-ers in next
Room, Who were entred into a strong
debate concerning ye Signifycation of
the name of their Country, (*viz.*) *Nar-
raganset.* One said it was named so by
ye Indians, because there grew a Brier
there, of a prodigious Highth and big-
ness, the like hardly ever known, called
by the Indians Narragansett; And quotes
an Indian of so Barberous a name for
his Author, that I could not write it.
His Antagonist Replyed no——It was
from a Spring it had its name, wch hee
well knew where it was, which was ex-
treem

treem cold in summer, and as Hott as
could be imagined in the winter, which
was much resorted too by the natives,
and by them called Narragansett, (Hott
and Cold,) and that was the originall
of their places name——with a thousand
Impertinances not worth notice, w^ch
He utter'd with such a Roreing voice
and Thundering blows with the fist of
wickedness on the Table, that it peirced
my very head. I heartily fretted, and
wish't 'um tongue tyed; but wth as little
succes as a freind of mine once, who
was (as shee said) kept a whole night
awake, on a Jorny, by a country Left.
and a Sergent, Insigne and a Deacon,
contriving how to bring a triangle into
a Square. They kept calling for tother
Gill, wch while they were swallowing,
was some Intermission; But presently,
like Oyle to fire, encreased the flame.
I set my Candle on a Chest by the bed
                                    side,

side, and setting up, fell to my old way of composing my Resentments, in the following manner:

> I ask thy Aid, O Potent Rum!
> To Charm these wrangling Topers Dum.
> Thou hast their Giddy Brains possest—
> The man confounded wth the Beast—
> And I, poor I, can get no rest.
> Intoxicate them with thy fumes:
> O still their Tongues till morning comes!

And I know not but my wishes took effect; for the dispute soon ended w^th 'tother Dram; and so Good night!

❀❀❀❀❀❀❀❀❀❀❀❀❀❀❀❀❀❀❀

Wedensday, Octob^r 4th.

About four in the morning, we set out for Kingston (for so was the Town called) with a french Docter in our company. Hee and ye Post put on very furiously, so that I could not keep up with them, only as now and then they'd stop

ſtop till they see mee. This Rode was poorly furnished wᵗʰ accommodations for Travellers, so that we were forced to ride 22 miles by the poſt's account, but neerer thirty by mine, before wee could bait so much as our Horses, wᶜʰ I exceedingly complained of. But the poſt encourag'd mee, by saying wee should be well accommodated anon at mr. Devills, a few miles further. But I queſtioned whether we ought to go to the Devil to be helpt out of affliction. However, like the reſt of Deluded souls that poſt to yᵉ Infernal denn, Wee made all posible speed to this Devil's Habitation; where alliting, in full assurance of good accommodation, wee were going in. But meeting his two daughters, as I suposed twins, they so neerly resembled each other, both in features and habit, and look't as old as the Divel himselfe, and quite as Ugly,

We

We desired entertainm't, but could hardly get a word out of 'um, till with our Importunity, telling them our necesity, &c. they call'd the old Sophister, who was as sparing of his words as his daughters had bin, and no, or none, was the reply's hee made us to our demands. Hee differed only in this from the old fellow in to'ther Country: hee let us depart. However, I thought it proper to warn poor Travailers to endeavor to Avoid falling into circumstances like ours, wch at our next Stage I sat down and did as followeth:

> May all that dread the cruel feind of night
> Keep on, and not at this curs't Mansion light.
> 'Tis Hell; 'tis Hell! and Devills here do dwell:
> Here dwells the Devill—surely this's Hell.
> Nothing but Wants: a drop to cool yo'r Tongue
> Cant be procur'd these cruel Feinds among.
> Plenty of horrid Grins and looks sevear,
> Hunger and thirst, But pitty's bannish'd here—
> The Right hand keep, if Hell on Earth you fear!

Thus

Thus leaving this habitation of cruelty, we went forward; and arriving at an Ordinary about two mile further, found tollerable accommodation. But our Hostes, being a pretty full mouth'd old creature, entertain'd our fellow travailer, yᵉ french Docter wᵗʰ Inumirable complaints of her bodily infirmities; and whisperd to him so lou'd, that all yᵉ House had as full a hearing as hee: which was very divirting to yᵉ company, (of which there was a great many,) as one might see by their sneering. But poor weary I slipt out to enter my mind in my Jornal, and left my Great Landly with her Talkative Guests to themselves.

From hence we proceeded (about ten forenoon) through the Narragansett country, pretty Leisurely; and about one afternoon come to Paukataug River, wᶜʰ was about two hundred paces over
                                                                over

over, and now very high, and no way
over to to'ther side but this. I darid not
venture to Ride thro, my courage at
beſt in such cases but small, And now
at the Loweſt Ebb, by reason of my
weary, very weary, hungry and uneasy
Circumſtances. So takeing leave of my
company, tho' wth no little Reluctance,
that I could not proceed wth them on
my Jorny, Stop at a little cottage Juſt
by the River, to wait the Waters falling,
wch the old man that lived there said
would be in a little time, and he would
conduct me safe over. This little Hutt
was one of the wretchedeſt I ever saw
a habitation for human creatures. It
was suported with shores enclosed with
Clapbords, laid on Lengthways, and
so much asunder, that the Light come
throu' every where; the doore tyed on
wth a cord in ye place of hinges; The
floor the bear earth; no windows but
such

such as the thin covering afforded, nor
any furniture but a Bedd wth a glass
Bottle hanging at ye head on't; an
earthan cupp, a small pewter Bason, A
Bord wth ſticks to ſtand on, inſtead of
a table, and a block or two in ye corner
inſtead of chairs. The family were the
old man, his wife and two Children;
all and every part being the picture
of poverty. Notwithſtanding both the
Hutt and its Inhabitance were very
clean and tydee: to the crossing the
Old Proverb, that bare walls make gid-
dy hows-wifes.

I Bleſt myselfe that I was not one of
this misserable crew; and the Impressions their wretchedness formed in me
caused mee on ye very Spott to say:

Tho' Ill at ease, A stranger and alone,
All my fatigu's shall not extort a grone.
These Indigents have hunger wth their ease;
Their best is wors behalfe then my disease.
Their Misirable hutt wch Heat and Cold
                                    Alternately

Alternately without Repulse do hold;
Their Lodgings thyn and hard, their Indian fare,
The mean Apparel which the wretches wear,
And their ten thousand ills wch can't be told,
Makes nature er'e 'tis midle age'd look old.
When I reflect, my late fatigues do seem
Only a notion or forgotten Dreem.

I had scarce done thinking, when an Indian-like Animal come to the door, on a creature very much like himselfe, in mien and feature, as well as Ragged cloathing; and having 'litt, makes an Awkerd Scratch wth his Indian shoo, and a Nodd, sitts on ye block, fumbles out his black Junk, dipps it in ye Ashes, and presents it piping hott to his mus-cheeto's, and fell to sucking like a calf, without speaking, for near a quarter of an hower. At length the old man said how do's Sarah do? who I understood was the wretches wife, and Daughter to ye old man: he Replyed—as well as can be expected, &c. So I remembered the

the old say, and suposed I knew Sarah's case. Butt hee being, as I understood, going over the River, as ugly as hee was, I was glad to ask him to show me ye way to Saxtons, at Stoningtown; wch he promising, I ventur'd over wth the old mans assistance; who having rewarded to content, with my Tatter-tailed guide, I Ridd on very slowly thro' Stoningtown, where the Rode was very Stony and uneven. I asked the fellow, as we went, divers questions of the place and way, &c. I being arrived at my country Saxtons, at Stonington, was very well accommodated both as to vic-tuals and Lodging, the only Good of both I had found since my setting out. Here I heard there was an old man and his Daughter to come that way, bound to N. London; and being now destitute of a Guide, gladly waited for them, being in so good a harbour, and accordingly,

Thirsday,

Thirsday, Octobr ye 5th,

about 3 in the afternoon, I sat forward
with neighbor Polly and Jemima, a Girl
about 18 Years old, who hee said he had
been to fetch out of the Narragansetts,
and said they had Rode thirty miles
that day, on a sory lean Jade, wth only a
Bagg under her for a pillion, which the
poor Girl often complain'd was very
uneasy.

Wee made Good speed along, w^{ch}
made poor Jemima make many a sow'r
face, the mare being a very hard trot-
ter; and after many a hearty and bitter
Oh, she at length Low'd out: Lawful
Heart father! this bare mare hurts mee
Dingeely, I'me direfull sore I vow;
with many words to that purpose: poor
Child sais Gaffer—she us't to serve your
mother

mother so. I don't care how mother us't to do, quoth Jemima, in a pasionate tone. At which the old man Laught, and kik't his Jade o' the side, which made her Jolt ten times harder.

About seven that Evening, we come to New London Ferry: here, by reason of a very high wind, we mett with great difficulty in getting over—the Boat tos't exceedingly, and our Horses capper'd at a very surprizing Rate, and set us all in a fright; especially poor Jemima, who desired her father to say so jack to the Jade, to make her ſtand. But the careless parent, taking no notice of her repeated desires, She Rored out in a Passionate manner: Pray suth father, Are you deaf? Say so Jack to the Jade, I tell you. The Dutiful Parent obey's; saying so Jack, so Jack, as gravely as if hee'd bin to saying Catechise after Young Miss, who with her fright look't of all coullors in yᵉ RainBow.

Being

Being safely arrived at the house of
Mrs. Prentices in N. London, I treated
neighbour Polly and daughter for their
divirting company, and bid them fare-
well; and between nine and ten at night
waited on the Rev^d Mr. Gurdon Salton-
ſtall, miniſter of the town, who kindly
Invited me to Stay that night at his
house, where I was very handsomely
and plentifully treated and Lodg'd; and
made good the Great Charaĉter I had
before heard concerning him : *viz.* that
hee was the moſt affable, courteous,
Genero's and beſt of men.

Friday, *Oĉto^r 6th.*

I got up very early, in Order to hire
somebody to go with mee to New Haven, being in Great parplexity at the
thoughts of proceeding alone; which
my

my moſt hospitable entertainer observing, himselfe went, and soon return'd wth a young Gentleman of the town, who he could confide in to Go with mee; and about eight this morning, wth Mr. Joshua Wheeler my new Guide, takeing leave of this worthy Gentleman, Wee advanced on towards Seabrook. The Rodes all along this way are very bad, Incumbred wth Rocks and mountainos passages, wch were very disagreeable to my tired carcass; but we went on with a moderate pace wch made ye Journy more pleasent. But after about eight miles Rideing, in going over a Bridge under wch the River Run very swift, my hors ſtumbled, and very narrowly 'scaped falling over into the water; wch extreemly frightened mee. But through God's Goodness I met with no harm, and mounting agen, in about half a miles Rideing, come to an ordinary,

ordinary, were well entertained by a woman of about seventy and vantage, but of as Sound Intellectuals as one of seventeen. Shee entertain'd Mr. Wheeler wth some passages of a Wedding awhile ago at a place hard by, the Brides-Groom being about her Age or something above, Saying his Children was dredfully against their fathers marrying, wch she condemned them extreemly for.

From hence wee went pretty briskly forward, and arriv'd at Saybrook ferry about two of the Clock afternoon; and crossing it, wee call'd at an Inn to Bait, (foreseeing we should not have such another Opportunity till we come to Killingsworth.) Landlady come in, with her hair about her ears, and hands at full pay scratching. Shee told us shee had some mutton wch shee would broil, wch I was glad to hear; But I supose forgot to

to wash her scratchers; in a little time
shee brot it in; but it being pickled,
and my Guide said it smelt ſtrong of
head sause, we left it, and pᵈ sixpence
a piece for our Dinners, wᶜʰ was only
smell.

So wee putt forward with all speed,
and about seven at night come to Killingsworth, and were tollerably well
with Travillers fare, and Lodgd there
that night.

✻✻✻✻✻✻✻✻✻✻✻✻✻✻✻✻✻✻✻✻✻✻✻

Saturday, Oɛt. 7th,

we sett out early in the Morning, and
being something unaquainted wᵗʰ the
way, having ask't it of some wee mett,
they told us wee muſt Ride a mile or
two and turne down a Lane on the
Right hand; and by their Direɛtion
wee Rode on but not Yet comeing to
yᵉ

yᵉ turning, we mett a Young fellow
and ask't him how farr it was to the
Lane which turn'd down towards Guil-
ford. Hee said wee muſt Ride a little
further, and turn down by the Corner
of uncle Sams Lott. My Guide vented
his Spleen at the Lubber; and we soon
after came into the Rhode, and keeping
ſtill on, without any thing further Re-
markabell, about two a clock afternoon
we arrived at New Haven, where I was
received with all Posible Respeᒍts and
civility. Here I discharged Mr. Wheeler with a reward to his satisfaᒍtion, and
took some time to reſt after so long and
toilsome a Journey; and Inform'd myselfe of the manners and cuſtoms of the
place, and at the same time employed
myselfe in the afair I went there upon.

They are Govern'd by the same Laws
as wee in Boſton, (or little differing,)
thr'out this whole Colony of Conneᒍt-
icot,

icot, And much the same way of Church Government, and many of them good, Sociable people, and I hope Religious too: but a little too much Independant in their principalls, and, as I have been told, were formerly in their Zeal very Riggid in their Administrations towards such as their Lawes made Offenders, even to a harmless Kiss or Innocent merriment among Young people. Whipping being a frequent and counted an easy Punishment, about wch as other Crimes, the Judges were absolute in their Sentences. They told mee a pleasant Story about a pair of Justices in those parts, wch I may not omit the relation of.

A negro Slave belonging to a man in ye Town, Stole a hogs head from his master, and gave or sold it to an Indian, native of the place. The Indian sold it in the neighbourhood, and so the theft

was

was found out. Thereupon the Heathen was Seized, and carried to the Justices House to be Examined. But his worship (it seems) was gone into the feild, with a Brother in office, to gather in his Pompions. Whither the malefactor is hurried, And Complaint made, and satisfaction in the name of Justice demanded. Their Worships cann't proceed in form without a Bench : whereupon they Order one to be Imediately erected, which, for want of fitter materials, they made with pompions— which being finished, down setts their Worships, and the Malefactor call'd, and by the Senior Justice Interrogated after the following manner. You Indian why did You steal from this man? You sho'dn't do so—it's a Grandy wicked thing to steal. Hol't Hol't cryes Justice Jun.ᵣ Brother, You speak negro to him. I'le ask him. You sirrah, why
did

did You steal this man's Hoggshead?
Hoggshead? (replys the Indian,) me
no stomany. No? says his Worship;
and pulling off his hatt, Patted his own
head with his hand, sais, Tatapa—You,
Tatapa—you; all one this. Hoggshead
all one this. Hah! says Netop, now me
stomany that. Whereupon the Company fell into a great fitt of Laughter,
even to Roreing. Silence is comanded,
but to no effect: for they continued per-
fectly Shouting. Nay, sais his worship,
in an angry tone, if it be so, *take mee off
the Bench.*

Their Diversions in this part of the
Country are on Lecture days and Training days mostly: on the former there
is Riding from town to town.

And on training dayes The Youth
divert themselves by Shooting at the
Target, as they call it, (but it very much
resembles a pillory,) where hee that
hitts

hitts neerest the white has some yards of Red Ribbin presented him wch being tied to his hattband, the two ends streeming down his back, he is Led away in Triumph, wth great applause, as the winners of the Olympiack Games. They generally marry very young: the males oftener as I am told under twentie than above; they generally make public wedings, and have a way something singular (as they say) in some of them, *viz*. Just before Joyning hands the Bridegroom quitts the place, who is soon followed by the Bridesmen, and as it were, dragg'd back to duty—being the reverse to ye former practice among us, to steal m^s Pride.

There are great plenty of Oysters all along by the sea side, as farr as I Rode in the Collony, and those very good. And they Generally lived very well and comfortably in their famelies. But too Indulgent

dulgent (especially ye farmers) to their slaves: sufering too great familiarity from them, permitting y^m to sit at Table and eat with them, (as they say to save time,) and into the dish goes the black hoof as freely as the white hand. They told me that there was a farmer lived nere the Town where I lodgd who had some difference wth his slave, concerning something the master had promised him and did not punctualy perform; wch caused some hard words between them; But at length they put the matter to Arbitration and Bound themselves to stand to the award of such as they named——wch done, the Arbitrators Having heard the Allegations of both parties, Order the master to pay 40^s to black face, and acknowledge his fault. And so the matter ended: the poor master very honestly standing to the award.

There

There are every where in the Towns as I passed, a Number of Indians the Natives of the Country, and are the moſt salvage of all the salvages of that kind that I had ever Seen: little or no care taken (as I heard upon enquiry) to make them otherwise. They have in some places Landes of their owne, and Govern'd by Law's of their own making;—they marry many wives and at pleasure put them away, and on the leaſt dislike or fickle humour, on either side, saying *ſtand away* to one another is a sufficient Divorce. And indeed those uncomely *Stand aways* are too much in Vougue among the English in this (Indulgent Colony) as their Records plentifully prove, and that on very trivial matters, of which some have been told me, but are not proper to be Related by a Female pen, tho some of that foolish sex have had too large a share in the ſtory.

If

If the natives committ any crime on their own precincts among themselves, ye English takes no Cognezens of. But if on the English ground, they are punishable by our Laws. They mourn for their Dead by blacking their faces, and cutting their hair, after an Awkerd and frightfull manner; But can't bear You should mention the names of their dead Relations to them: they trade most for Rum, for wch they^d hazzard their very lives; and the English fit them Generally as well, by seasoning it plentifully with water.

They give the title of merchant to every trader; who Rate their Goods according to the time and spetia they pay in: *viz.* Pay, mony, Pay as mony, and trusting. *Pay* is Grain, Pork, Beef, &c. at the prices sett by the General Court that Year; *mony* is pieces of Eight, Ryalls, or Boston or Bay shillings (as they

they call them,) or Good hard money,
as sometimes silver coin is termed by
them; also Wampom, *viz*ᵗ· Indian beads
wᶜʰ serves for change. *Pay as mony* is
provisions, as aforesᵈ one Third cheap-
er then as the Assembly or Geneˡ Court
sets it; and *Trust* as they and the merchᵗ
agree for time.

Now, when the buyer comes to ask
for a comodity, sometimes before the
merchant answers that he has it, he sais,
is Your pay redy? Perhaps the Chap Reply's Yes: what do You pay in? say's
the merchant. The buyer having answered, then the price is set; as suppose
he wants a sixpenny knife, in pay it is
12d—in pay as money eight pence, and
hard money its own price, *viz*. 6d. It
seems a very Intricate way of trade and
what *Lex Mercatoria* had not thought of.

Being at a merchants house, in comes
a tall country fellow, wᵗʰ his alfogeos
full

full of Tobacco; for they seldom Loose their Cudd, but keep Chewing and Spitting as long as they'r eyes are open,— he advanc't to the midle of the Room, makes an Awkward Nodd, and spitting a Large deal of Aromatick Tincture, he gave a scrape with his shovel like shoo, leaving a small shovel full of dirt on the floor, made a full ſtop, Hugging his own pretty Body with his hands under his arms, Stood ſtaring rown'd him, like a Catt let out of a Baskett. At laſt, like the creature Balaam Rode on, he opened his mouth and said : have You any Ribinen for Hatbands to sell I pray ? The Questions and Answers about the pay being paſt, the Ribin is bro't and opened. Bumpkin Simpers, cryes its confounded Gay I vow; and beckning to the door, in comes Jone Tawdry, dropping about 50 curtsees, and ſtands by him : hee shows her the Ribin. *Law You*, sais shee,

shee, *its right Gent*, do You, take it, *tis dreadfull pretty*. Then she enquires, *have You any hood silk I pray?* wch being brought and bought, Have You any *thred silk to sew it w^{th}* says shee, wch being accomodated wth they Departed. They Generaly ſtand after they come in a great while speachless, and sometimes dont say a word till they are askt what they want, which I Impute to the Awe they ſtand in of the merchants, who they are conſtantly almost Indebted too; and muſt take what they bring without Liberty to choose for themselves; but they serve them as well, making the merchants ſtay long enough for their pay.

We may Observe here the great necessity and bennifitt both of Education and Conversation; for these people have as Large a portion of mother witt, and sometimes a Larger, than those who have bin brought up in Citties; But for
want

want of emprovements, Render themselves almoſt Ridiculos, as above. I should
be glad if they would leave such follies,
and am sure all that Love Clean Houses
(at leaſt) would be glad on't too.

They are generaly very plain in their
dress, throuout all yᵉ Colony, as I saw,
and follow one another in their modes ;
that You may know where they belong,
especially the women, meet them where
you will.

Their Cheif Red Letter day is St. Elec-
tion, wᶜʰ is annualy Observed according to Charter, to choose their Govenʳ :
a blessing they can never be thankfull
enough for, as they will find, if ever it
be their hard fortune to loose it. The
present Govenor in Coneƈticott is the
Honᵇˡᵉ John Winthrop Esq. A Gentleman of an Ancient and Honourable
Family, whose Father was Govenor
here sometime before, and his Grand
father

father had bin Govr of the Massachusetts. This gentleman is a very curteous
and afable person, much Given to Hos-
pitality, and has by his Good services
Gain'd the affection of the people as
much as any who had bin before him
in that post.

Decr 6th.

'Being by this time well Recruited
and rested after my Journy, my business
lying unfinished by some concerns at
New York depending thereupon, my
Kinsman, Mr. Thomas Trowbridge of
New Haven, must needs take a Journy
there before it could be accomplished,
I resolved to go there in company w^th
him, and a man of the town wch I en-
gaged to wait on me there. Accordingly, Dec. 6th we set out from New Haven,
and

and about 11 same morning came to Stratford ferry; wch crossing, about two miles on the other side Baited our horses and would have eat a morsell ourselves, But the Pumpkin and Indian mixt Bred had such an Aspect, and the Bare-legg'd Punch so awkerd or rather Awfull a sound, that we left both, and proceeded forward, and about seven at night come to Fairfield, where we met with good entertainment and Lodg'd; and early next morning set forward to Norowalk, from its halfe Indian name *North-walk*, when about 12 at noon we arrived, and Had a Dinner of Fryed Venison, very savoury. Landlady wanting some pepper in the seasoning, bid the Girl hand her the spice in the little *Gay* cupp on ye shelfe. From hence we Hasted towards Rye, walking and Leading our Horses neer a mile together, up a prodigios high Hill; and so Riding till about nine at

night,

night, and there arrived and took up our
Lodgings at an ordinary, wch a French
family kept. Here being very hungry, I
desired a fricasee, wch the Frenchman
undertakeing, mannaged so contrary to
my notion of Cookery, that I haſtned to
Bed superless; And being shewd the way
up a pair of ſtairs wᶜʰ had such a narrow
passage that I had almoſt ſtopt by the
Bulk of my Body; But arriving at my
apartment found it to be a little Lento
Chamber furnisht amongſt other Rub-
bish with a High Bedd and a Low one,
a Long Table, a Bench and a Bottom-
less chair,——Little Miss went to scratch
up my Kennell wᶜʰ Russelled as if shee'd
bin in the Barn amongſt the Husks, and
supose such was the contents of the tick-
in——nevertheless being exceeding weary, down I laid my poor Carkes (never
more tired) and found my Covering as
scanty as my Bed was hard. Annon I
                                    heard

heard another Russelling noise in Y^e
Room—called to know the matter—
Little miss said shee was making a bed
for the men; who, when they were in
Bed, complained their leggs lay out of
it by reason of its shortness—my poor
bones complained bitterly not being
used to such Lodgings, and so did the
man who was with us; and poor I made
but one Grone, which was from the
time I went to bed to the time I Riss,
which was about three in the morning,
Setting up by the Fire till Light, and
having discharged our ordinary wch was
as dear as if we had had far better fare—
wee took our leave of Monsier and a-
bout seven in the morn come to New
Rochell a french town, where we had a
good Breakfaſt. And in the ſtrength of
that about an how'r before sunsett got
to York. Here I applyd myself to Mr.
Burroughs, a merchant to whom I was
recommended

recommended by my Kinsman Capt. Prout, and received great Civilities from him and his spouse, who were now both Deaf but very agreeable in their Conversation, Diverting me with pleasant Stories of their knowledge in Brittan from whence they both come, one of which was above the rest very pleasant to me *viz.* my Lord Darcy had a very extravagant Brother who had mortgaged what Estate hee could not sell, and in good time dyed leaving only one son. Him his Lordship (having none of his own) took and made him Heir of his whole Estate, which he was to receive at the death of his Aunt. He and his Aunt in her widowhood held a right understanding and lived as become such Relations, shee being a discreat Gentlewoman and he an Ingenios Young man. One day Hee fell into some Company though far his inferiors, very freely told him

him of the Ill circumſtances his fathers
Eſtate lay under, and the many Debts he
left unpaid to the wrong of poor people with whom he had dealt. The Young
gentleman was put out of countenance
—no way hee could think of to Redress
himself—his whole dependance being
on the Lady his Aunt, and how to speak
to her he knew not—Hee went home,
sat down to dinner and as usual sometimes with her when the Chaplain was
absent, she desired him to say Grace, w^ch
he did after this manner:

> Pray God in Mercy take my Lady Darcy
> Unto his Heavenly Throne,
> That Little John may live like a man,
> And pay every man his own.

The prudent Lady took no present notice, But finishd dinner, after wch having sat and talk't awhile (as Cuſtomary)
He Riss, took his Hatt and Going out she
desired him to give her leave to speak to
him

him in her Clossett, Where being come
she desired to know why hee prayed
for her Death in the manner aforesaid,
and what part of her deportment towards him merritted such desires. Hee
Reply'd, none at all, But he was under
such disadvantages that nothing but
that could do him service, and told her
how he had been affronted as above, and
what Impressions it had made upon
him. The Lady made him a gentle repri-
mand that he had not informed her after
another manner, Bid him see what his
father owed and he should have money
to pay it to a penny, And always to lett
her know his wants and he should have
a redy supply. The Young Gentleman
charm'd with his Aunts Discrete man-
agement, Beggd her pardon and accept-
ed her kind offer and retrieved his fathers
Estate, &c. and said Hee hoped his Aunt
would never dye, for shee had done better

ter by him than hee could have done for himself.—Mr. Burroughs went with me to Vendue where I bought about 100 Rheem of paper wch was retaken in a fly-boat from Holland and sold very Reasonably here—some ten, some Eight shillings per Rheem by the Lott wch was ten Rheem in a Lott. And at the Vendue I made a great many acquaintances amongst the good women of the town, who curteosly invited me to their houses and generously entertained me.

The Cittie of New York is a pleasant, well compacted place, situated on a Commodius River wch is a fine harbour for shipping. The Buildings Brick Generaly, very stately and high, though not altogether like ours in Boston. The Bricks in some of the Houses are of divers Coullers and laid in Checkers, being glazed look very agreeable. The inside of them are neat to admiration, the wooden

wooden work, for only the walls are
plaſterd, and the Sumers and Giſt are
plained and kept very white scowr'd as
so is all the partitions if made of Bords.
The fire places have no Jambs (as ours
have) But the Backs run flush with the
walls, and the Hearth is of Tyles and is
as farr out into the Room at the Ends as
before the fire, wch is Generally Five foot
in the Low'r rooms, and the peice over
where the mantle tree should be is made
as ours with Joyners work, and as I supose is faſten'd to iron rodds inside.
The House where the Vendue was, had
Chimney Corners like ours, and they and
the hearths were laid wth the fineſt tile
that I ever see, and the ſtair cases laid all
with white tile which is ever clean, and
so are the walls of the Kitchen wch had
a Brick floor. They were making Great
preparations to Receive their Govenor,
Lord Cornbury from the Jerseys, and
for

for that End raised the militia to Gard him on shore to the fort.

They are Generaly of the Church of England and have a New England Gentleman for their minister, and a very fine church set out with all Customary requsites. There are also a Dutch and Divers Conventicles as they call them, *viz.* Baptist, Quakers, &c. They are not strict in keeping the Sabbath as in Boston and other places where I had bin, But seem to deal with great exactness as farr as I see or Deall with. They are sociable to one another and Curteos and Civill to strangers and fare well in their houses. The English go very fasheonable in their dress. But the Dutch, especially the middling sort, differ from our women, in their habitt go loose, were French muches wch are like a Capp and a head band in one, leaving their ears bare, which are sett out wth Jewells of a large size and

and many in number. And their fingers
hoop't with Rings, some with large
Stones in them of many Coullers as were
their pendants in their ears, which You
should see very old women wear as well
as Young.

They have Vendues very frequently
and make their Earnings very well by
them, for they treat with good Liquor
Liberally, and the Customers Drink as
Liberally and Generally pay for't as well,
by paying for that which they Bidd up
Briskly for, after the sack has gone plentifully about, tho' sometimes good penny worths are got there. Their Diversions in the Winter is Riding Sleys about
three or four Miles out of Town, where
they have Houses of entertainment at a
place called the Bowery, and some go
to friends Houses who handsomely treat
them. Mr. Burroughs cary'd his spouse
and Daughter and myself out to one
Madame

Madame Dowes, a Gentlewoman that lived at a farm House, who gave us a handsome Entertainment of five or six Dishes and choice Beer and metheglin, Cyder, &c. all which she said was the produce of her farm. I believe we mett 50 or 60 slays that day—they fly with great swiftness and some are so furious that they'le turn out of the path for none except a Loaden Cart. Nor do they spare for any diversion the place affords, and sociable to a degree, they'r Tables being as free to their Naybours as to themselves.

Having here transacted the affair I went upon and some other that fell in the way, after about a fortnight's stay there I left New-York with no Little regrett, and

✿✿✿✿✿✿✿✿✿✿✿✿✿✿✿✿✿✿✿✿✿✿✿

Thursday, Dec. 21,

set

set out for New Haven wth my Kinsman Trowbridge, and the man that
waited on me about one afternoon, and
about three come to half-way house
about ten miles out of town, where we
Baited and went forward, and about
5 come to Spiting Devil, Else Kings
bridge, where they pay three pence for
passing over with a horse, which the
man that keeps the Gate set up at the
end of the Bridge receives.

We hoped to reach the french town
and Lodg there that night, but unhapi-
ly lost our way about four miles short,
and being overtaken by a great storm of
wind and snow which set full in our
faces about dark, we were very uneasy.
But meeting one Gardner who lived in
a Cottage thereabout, offered us his fire
to set by, having but one poor Bedd,
and his wife not well, &c. or he would
go to a House with us, where he thought
we

we might be better accommodated—
thither we went, But a surly old shee
Creature, not worthy the name of woman, who would hardly let us go into
her Door, though the weather was so
Stormy none but she would have turnd
out a Dogg. But her son whose name
was gallop, who lived Just by Invited us
to his house and shewed me two pair of
Stairs, *viz.* one up the loft and tother up
the Bedd, wch was as hard as it was high,
and warmed it with a hott Stone at the
feet. I lay very uncomfortably, inso-
much that I was so very cold and sick I
was forced to call them up to give me
something to warm me. They had nothing but milk in the house, wch they
Boild, and to make it better sweetened
wth molasses, which I not knowing or
thinking oft till it was down and coming up agen wch it did in so plentifull a
manner that my host was soon paid dou-
ble

ble for his portion, and that in specia. But I believe it did me service in Cleering my ſtomach. So after this sick and weary night at Eaſt Cheſter, (a very miserable poor place,) the weather being now fair,

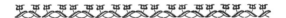

Friday the 22ᵈ Dec.

we set out for New Rochell, where being come we had good Entertainment and Recruited ourselves very well. This is a very pretty place well compaꜩ, and good handsome houses, Clean, good and passable Rodes, and situated on a Navigable River, abundance of land well fined and Cleerd all along as wee passed, which caused in me a Love to the place, wᶜʰ I could have been content to live in it. Here wee Ridd over a Bridge made of one entire ſtone of such

a

a Breadth that a cart might pass with safety, and to spare—it lay over a passage cutt through a Rock to convey water to a mill not farr off. Here are three fine Taverns within call of each other, very good provision for Travailers.

Thence we travailed through Merrinak, a neet, though little place, wth a navigable River before it, one of the pleasante&t I ever see—Here were good Buildings, Especialy one, a very fine seat, wch they told me was Col. Hethcoats, who I had heard was a very fine Gentleman. From hence we come to HorsNeck, where wee Baited, and they told me that one Church of England parson officiated in all these three towns once every Sunday in turns throughout the Year; and that they all could but poorly maintaine him which they grudg'd to do, being a poor and quarelsome crew as I under&tand by our Ho&t; their Quarelling about their

their choice of Minister, they chose to
have none—But caused the Government
to send this Gentleman to them. Here
wee took leave of York Government, and
Descending the Mountainos passage
that almost broke my heart in ascending
before, we come to Stamford, a well com-
pact Town, but miserable meeting house,
wch we passed, and thro' many and great
difficulties, as Bridges which were exceeding high and very tottering and of
vast Length, steep and Rocky Hills and
precipices, (Buggbears to a fearful female
travailer.) About nine at night we come
to Norrwalk, having crept over a tim-
ber of a Broken Bridge about thirty foot
long, and perhaps fifty to ye water. I was
exceeding tired and cold when we come
to our Inn, and could get nothing there
but poor entertainment, and the Imper-
tinant Bable of one of the worst of men,
among many others of which our Host
made

made one, who, had he bin one degree Impudenter, would have outdone his Grandfather. And this I think is the moſt perplexed night I have yet had. From hence,

❖❖❖❖❖❖❖❖❖❖❖❖❖❖❖❖❖❖❖❖

Saturday, Dec. 23,

a very cold and windy day, after an Intolerable night's Lodging, wee haſted forward only observing in our way the Town to be situated on a Navigable river wth indiferent Buildings and people more refined than in some of the country towns wee had passed, tho' vicious enough, the Church and Tavern being next neighbours. Having Ridd thro a difficult River we come to Fairfield where wee Baited and were much refreshed as well with the Good things wch gratified our appetites as the time took to reſt our wearied Limbs, wch Latter I employed in in enquiring concerning the Town and manners of the people, &c. This is a considerable town, and filld as they say with wealthy people—have a spacious meeting house and good Buildings. But the Inhabitants are Litigious, nor do they well agree with their minister, who (they say) is a very worthy Gentleman.

They have aboundance of sheep, whose very Dung brings them great gain, with part of which they pay their Parsons sallery. And they Grudg that, prefering their Dung before their minister. They Lett out their sheep at so much as they agree upon for a night; the highest Bidder always caries them, And they will sufficiently Dung a Large quantity of Land before morning. But were once Bitt by a sharper who had them a night and sheared them all before morning—From hence we went to Stratford, the next Town, in which I observed

observed but few houses, and those not very good ones. But the people that I conversed with were civill and good natured. Here we ſtaid till late at night, being to cross a Dangerous River ferry, the River at that time full of Ice; but after about four hours waiting with great difficulty wee got over. My fears and fatigues prevented my here taking any particular observation. Being got to Milford, it being late in the night, I could go no further; my fellow travailer going forward, I was invited to Lodg at Mrs. —— ——, a very kind and civill Gentlewoman, by whom I was handsomely and kindly entertained till the next night. The people here go very plain in their apparel (more plain than I had observed in the towns I had passed) and seem to be very grave and serious. They told me there was a singing Quaker lived there, or at leaſt had a strong inclination

inclination to be so, His Spouse not at all affected that way. Some of the singing Crew come there one day to visit him, who being then abroad, they sat down (to the woman's no small vexation) Humming and singing and groneing after their conjuring way—Says the woman are you singing quakers? Yea says They—Then take my squalling Brat of a child here and sing to it says she for I have almost split my throat wth singing to him and cant get the Rogue to sleep. They took this as a great Indignity, and mediately departed. Shaking the dust from their Heels left the good woman and her Child among the number of the wicked.

This is a Seaport place and accomodated with a Good Harbour, But I had not opportunity to make particular observations because it was Sabbath day— This Evening,

December

✿ ✿

December 24,

I set out with the Gentlewomans son who she very civilly offered to go with me when she see no parswasions would cause me to stay which she pressingly desired, and crossing a ferry having but nine miles to New Haven in a short time arrived there and was Kindly received and well accommodated amongst my Friends and Relations.

The Government of Connecticut Collony begins westward towards York at Stanford (as I am told) and so runs Eastward towards Boston (I mean in my range, because I dont intent to extend my description beyond my own travails) and ends that way at Stonington—And has a great many Large towns lying more northerly. It is a plentiful Country for provisions of all sorts and its Generally Healthy.

Healthy. No one that can and will be dilligent in this place need fear poverty nor the want of food and Rayment.

January 6th.

Being now well Recruited and fitt for business I discoursed the persons I was concerned with, that we might finnish in order to my return to Boston. They delayd as they had hitherto done hoping to tire my Patience. But I was resolute to ſtay and see an End of the matter let it be never so much to my disadvantage —So January 9th they come again and promise the Wednesday following to go through with the diſtribution of the Eſtate which they delayed till Thursday and then come with new amusements. But at length by the mediation of that holy good Gentleman, the Rev. Mr. James

James Pierpont, the minister of New
Haven, and with the advice and assistance of other our Good friends we come
to an accommodation and distribution,
which having finished though not till
February, the man that waited on me to
York taking the charge of me I sit out
for Boston. We went from New Haven
upon the ice (the ferry being not passable thereby) and the Rev. Mr. Pierpont
wth Madam Prout Cuzin Trowbridge
and divers others were taking leave wee
went onward without any thing Re-
markabl till we come to New London
and Lodged again at Mr. Saltonstalls——
and here I dismist my Guide, and my
Generos entertainer provided me Mr.
Samuel Rogers of that place to go home
with me——I stayed a day here Longer
than I intended by the Commands of
the Honble Govenor Winthrop to stay
and take a supper with him whose won-
derful

derful civility I may not omitt. The next
morning I Crossed yᵉ Ferry to Groton,
having had the Honor of the Company,
of Madam Livingſton (who is the Gov-
enors Daughter) and Mary Chriſtophers
and divers others to the boat—And
that night Lodgᵈ at Stonington and had
RoſtBeef and pumpkin sause for supper.
The next night at Haven's and had Roſt
fowle, and the next day wee come to a
river which by Reason of Yᵉ Freshetts
coming down was swell'ᵈ so high wee
fearᵈ it impassable and the rapid stream
was very terryfying—However we muſt
over and that in a small Cannoo. Mr.
Rogers assuring me of his good Conduct, I after a ſtay of near an how'r on
the shore for consultation went into the
Cannoo, and Mr. Rogers paddled about
100 yards up the Creek by the shore
side, turned into the swift stream and
dexterously steering her in a moment
wee

wee come to the other side as swiftly passing as an arrow shott out of the Bow by
a strong arm. I staid on ye shore till Hee
returned to fetch our horses, which he
caused to swim over himself bringing
the furniture in the Cannoo. But it is
past my skill to express the Exceeding
fright all their transactions formed in
me. Wee were now in the colony of the
Massachusetts and taking Lodgings at
the first Inn we come to had a pretty difficult passage the next day which was
the second of March by reason of the
sloughy ways then thawed by the Sunn.
Here I mett Capt. John Richards of Boston who was going home, So being very
glad of his Company we Rode something harder than hitherto, and missing
my way in going up a very steep Hill, my
horse dropt down under me as Dead;
this new surprize no little hurt me meeting it Just at the Entrance into Dedham
from

from whence we intended to reach
home that night. But was now obliged
to gett another Hors there and leave
my own, resolving for Boſton that
night if possible. But in going over the
Causeway at Dedham the Bridge being
overflowed by the high waters com-
ming down I very narrowly escaped
falling over into the river Hors and all
wch twas almoſt a miracle I did not—
now it grew late in the afternoon and
the people having very much discour-
aged us about the sloughy way wch they
said wee should find very difficult and
hazardous it so wrought on mee being
tired and dispirited and disapointed of
my desires of going home that I agreed
to Lodg there that night wch wee did at
the house of one Draper, and the next
day being March 3d wee got safe home
to Boſton, where I found my aged and
tender mother and my Dear and only
Child

Child in good health with open arms
redy to receive me, and my Kind relations and friends flocking in to wel-
come mee and hear the ſtory of my
transactions and travails I having this
day bin five months from home and
now I cannot fully express my Joy and
Satisfaction. But desire sincearly to a-
dore my Great Benefactor for thus gra-
ciously carying forth and returning in
safety his unworthy handmaid.

Five hundred and twenty-five copies printed
at the press of William Edwin Rudge, New
York, in October, 1920.

APPLEWOOD BOOKS
BRINGING THE PAST ALIVE

TIMELESS ADVICE & ENTERTAINMENT
FROM AMERICANS WHO CAME BEFORE US

George Washington on Manners

Benjamin Franklin on Money

Lydia Maria Child on Raising Children

Henry David Thoreau on Walking

&

Many More Distinctive Classics

Now Available Again

At finer bookstores

& gift shops or from:

APPLEWOOD BOOKS
18 North Road
Bedford, MA 01730